Seymour Simon

SEE
MORE
READERS

COOL CARS

SeaStar Books • New York

Front cover photograph: This 1996 Hennessey Viper Venom 650R can go from 0 to 60 mph in 3.3 seconds.

Title page photograph: A Top Fuel dragster can go from 0 to 300 mph in less than 5 seconds.

This book is for my grandsons Joel and Benjamin.

Special thanks to reading consultant Dr. Linda B. Gambrell, Director, School of Education, Clemson University. Dr. Gambrell has served as President of the National Reading Conference and Board Member of the International Reading Association.

Permission to use the following photographs is gratefully acknowledged:
Front cover, pages 12–13: © Ron Kimball Studios; title page, pages 22–25: © Richard T. Bryant; pages 2–3: © EyeWire/Gettyimages; pages 4–5: © Deutsches Museum Munich; pages 6–7: © Bettmann/Corbis; pages 8–9: © Richard Lentinello; pages 10–11: © VW Trends Magazine; pages 14–15: © R.E. Pelham/Bruce Coleman; pages 16–17: © Yann Arthus Bertrand/Corbis; pages 18–19: © Reuters NewMedia Inc./Corbis; pages 20–21: © AFP/Corbis; pages 26–27, back cover: © David Madison Sports Images; pages 28–29: © Insurance Institute for Highway Safety; pages 30–31: © Justin Sullivan/Getty Images; page 32: © Mark E. Gibson/Corbis.

Library of Congress Cataloging-in-Publication Data is available.
ISBN 1-58717-236-4 (reinforced trade edition)
1 3 5 7 9 RTE 10 8 6 4 2
ISBN 1-58717-237-2 (paperback edition)
1 3 5 7 9 PB 10 8 6 4 2
PRINTED IN BELGIUM
For more information about our books, and the authors and artists who create them,
visit our web site: www.northsouth.com

In America, cars travel 2.5 trillion miles in a year. That's like going back and forth to the moon 5 million times.

Early motorcars were like bicycles with engines. This 1886 Benz car had three wire wheels and a seat for two. You can run faster than this car could move.

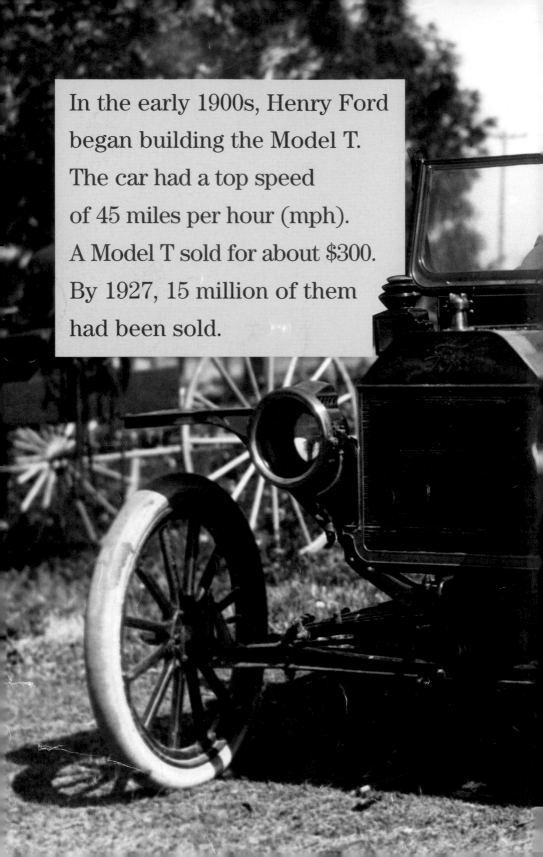

In the early 1900s, Henry Ford began building the Model T. The car had a top speed of 45 miles per hour (mph). A Model T sold for about $300. By 1927, 15 million of them had been sold.

The 1970 Chevrolet Corvette Stingray looked like a shark. It could go from 0 to 60 mph in less than six seconds.

With a top speed of 150 mph,
the Stingray was the fastest
American sports car you could buy.

The VW Beetle was not very fast or very big, but it got people where they wanted to go.
Everyone knew the Beetle shape.

Over 20 million VW Beetles were
sold between 1945 and 1978.
It is still the world's best-selling car.

The best-known luxury car ever made is the Rolls-Royce. Each one takes up to three months to build by hand. This 1960 Silver Cloud sold for more than ten VW Beetles.

A Rolls-Royce is so quiet inside that you can hear the sound of its clock ticking when you're driving.

Before Jeeps, the two rear wheels
pushed most cars forward.
But a Jeep's engine powers
both the front wheels
and the rear wheels.
Four-wheel drive cars move easily
through deep snow or mud
and over rocks or logs.

Rally cars are made to race on rough roads and in bad weather. The drivers sit inside a steel cage that protects them if the car rolls over. This car raced over 6,500 miles in the world-famous race from Paris, France, to Dakar in Senegal, Africa.

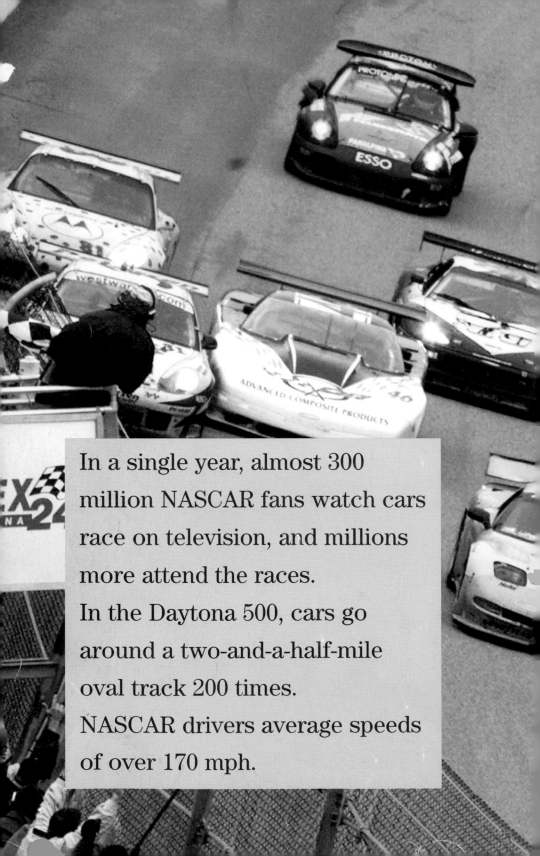

In a single year, almost 300 million NASCAR fans watch cars race on television, and millions more attend the races.

In the Daytona 500, cars go around a two-and-a-half-mile oval track 200 times.

NASCAR drivers average speeds of over 170 mph.

In a Formula One race, this Ferrari has to go both fast and slowly along the narrow, winding streets. Roaring down a straightaway, the Ferrari can go over 170 mph. But on a hairpin curve, the car has to slow down to 30 mph or it will spin out of control.

An Indianapolis 500 car has
a 750 horsepower engine
just behind the driver.
Indy cars can go over 250 mph on
the long straightaways in the race.

Seven crew members change
all four tires and refuel the car
in less than 20 seconds.

Drag cars race side by side
on a track only one-quarter
of a mile long.
Some drag-racing cars
can reach 300 mph
in less than four seconds.

These cars are so fast that
they need a parachute to
help them stop.

The fastest car in the world
is the Thrust SSC.
Like a jet airplane, it can travel
faster than the speed of sound.
Once, it reached a speed of
over 766 mph on a special track
in the Nevada desert.

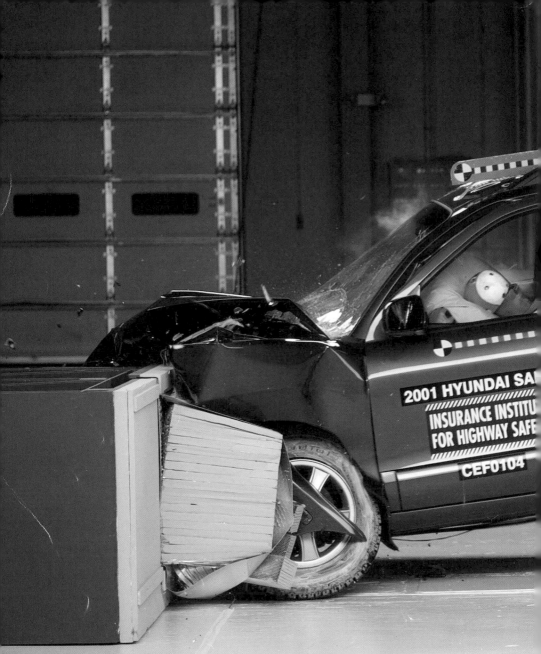

Engineers test the safety of cars
by crashing them into barriers.
They study what damage happens
to dummies inside the cars.

Modern cars have seat belts and
airbags to help prevent injury
in a car crash.
But good driver training and good
roads are also important for safety.

Governments pass laws to try to
cut down pollution caused by cars.
Electric cars that run on batteries
may be one answer to less pollution.

Cars have changed the way
the world looks and moves.